A PICTURE BOOK OF
DWIGHT DAVID EISENHOWER

DAVID A. ADLER

Holiday House / New York

"*A Picture Book of Dwight David Eisenhower* brings a true American hero to the attention of young children in search of a positive role model. The Eisenhower Foundation gives its highest recommendation to this entertaining and factual pictorial biography."
—Lynda Scheele, Executive Director, The Eisenhower Foundation

For Kim Barbieri,
Many thanks for your help, encouragement, and friendship

The photographs on page 25 are courtesy of the Arkansas History Commission.
The photograph on page 26 is courtesy of AP/Wide World Photos.
All other photographs are courtesy of the Dwight D. Eisenhower Library, Abilene, Kansas.

Library of Congress Cataloging-in-Publication Data
Adler, David A.
A picture book of Dwight David Eisenhower / by David A. Adler.— 1st ed.
p. cm.—(Picture book biography)
Summary: Details the life of the World War II general and
thirty-fourth president of the United States, Dwight Eisenhower.
Includes bibliographical references.
ISBN 0-8234-1702-6
1. Eisenhower, Dwight D. (Dwight David), 1890–1969—Juvenile literature.
2. Presidents—United States—Biography—Juvenile literature.
[1. Eisenhower, Dwight D. (Dwight David), 1890–1969. 2. Presidents.] I. Title.
E836 .A64 2002
973.921'092—dc21
[B]   2002017149

JACKET: YOUNG DWIGHT EISENHOWER ON A CAMPING TRIP. PAINTING BY DAN BROWN.

GENERAL EISENHOWER IN NEW YORK CITY, JUNE 19, 1945

It was Tuesday, June 19, 1945. Several million people had come to welcome General Dwight David Eisenhower to New York City. Thousands of schoolchildren had gathered along the streets. There were soldiers wearing their battle ribbons, marching bands, police on horseback and in cars, newsreel cameras, and a Navy blimp overhead.

AT CITY HALL

General Eisenhower stood in an open car, smiled, and waved to the cheering crowd. He had just returned from leading American and other Allied troops to victory in World War II over German forces in Europe. He was praised for his "brilliant leadership," courage, and determination. He was given a gold medal inscribed to "the victorious Commander in Chief of Allied Armies in defense of human liberty."

General Eisenhower blushed. "I'm just a Kansas farmer boy," he said, "who did his duty."

Dwight David Eisenhower was born on October 14, 1890. He was the third of seven sons of Ida and David Eisenhower. The Eisenhowers were a Kansas family but Dwight David was born in Denison, Texas, while the family briefly lived there. In 1892 the Eisenhowers returned to Kansas, to Abilene.

THE EISENHOWER FAMILY, 1902
FROM LEFT TO RIGHT, FRONT ROW, DAVID, MILTON, IDA; BACK ROW, DWIGHT, EDGAR, EARL, ARTHUR, ROY (ONE BROTHER, PAUL, DIED IN 1895.)

The family did for themselves. They smoked their own meats and dried their own fruits. Dwight's mother made and mended the family's clothes and linens. The boys did the laundry and ironing, and washed the dishes. They fed the animals, milked the cows, collected the eggs, picked the fruit, and tended the gardens. Dwight and his older brother Edgar took vegetables they grew and sold them door-to-door.

"I have found out in later years we were very poor," Dwight Eisenhower once said, "but the glory of America is that we didn't know it."

Dwight had a broad smile. He was friendly and popular in school. He and a few of his brothers were nicknamed "Ike," an adaptation of *Ei*, the first syllable in Eisenhower.

Dwight was an active boy. He loved sports.

One evening when he was fourteen, he raced some of his friends and fell. He scraped his knee and tore his pants, "a brand new pair of trousers," he remembered later, "of which I was exceedingly proud." Two days later his knee swelled and the swelling spread. "I dropped off," he later wrote, "into delirium." He was afraid he might lose his leg. He remembered saying, "I'd rather be dead than crippled and not be able to play ball."

ABILENE HIGH SCHOOL BASEBALL TEAM, 1908 EISENHOWER IS IN TOP ROW, SECOND FROM RIGHT.

After two weeks the swelling went down. After two months he was fully recovered. But he missed much of his freshman year of high school and had to repeat the grade.

Dwight had a logical mind and a good memory. He did well in spelling and mathematics, but his first love was history. George Washington was his hero. Dwight admired Washington's patience during troubled times, his courage and daring.

He graduated high school in 1909. He knew there was no money for college, so he wrote to his senator and asked to be appointed to a military academy, where he could get a free education. On June 14, 1911, he reported to the United States Military Academy at West Point, New York.

LETTER TO SENATOR BRISTOW

Abilene, Kansas,
Aug. 20, 1910.
Sen. Bristow,
Salina, Kans.
Dear Sir:
I would very much like to enter either the school at Annapolis, or the one at West Point. In order to do this, I must have an appointment to one of these places and so I am writing to you in order to secure the same.
I have graduated from high school and will be nineteen years of age this fall.
If you find it possible to appoint me to one of these schools, your kindness will certainly be appreciated by me.
Trusting to hear from you, concerning this matter, at your earliest convenience, I am,
Respectfully yours,
Dwight Eisenhower.

Dwight still loved sports. He hoped to
star on the Army football and baseball teams.
But in November 1912, first in a football
game and then in horse-riding exercises, he
badly hurt his knee. His dreams of athletic
glory were finished. "Life seemed to have little
meaning," he later wrote. "A need to excel was
almost gone." He even considered quitting the
Academy.

WEST POINT CADET AND FOOTBALL PLAYER, 1912

"I have often wondered why, at that moment, I did not give increased attention to studies," he later wrote. But he didn't. He was rebellious. "I was, in matters of discipline, far from a good cadet. . . . I enjoyed life in the Academy, had a good time with my pals."

Dwight Eisenhower's pals, the graduating class of 1915, did well in later military life. So many of them became generals that they have been called "the class the stars fell on."

WEST POINT GRADUATING CLASS, 1915

After graduation Eisenhower was assigned to the infantry at Fort Sam Houston, in Texas. There he met an "attractive girl, smaller than average, saucy in the look about her face and in her whole attitude," he later wrote. "That was the entrance into my life of Mamie Geneva Doud," the second of four daughters of John and Elivera Doud.

Dwight Eisenhower saw Mamie Doud whenever he could. He took her to dinners of chili, tamales, and enchiladas at a nearby Mexican restaurant and to music and comedy shows at the local vaudeville house. They married on July 1, 1916.

NEWLYWEDS DWIGHT AND MAMIE EISENHOWER, 1916

In 1917 Dwight and Mamie Eisenhower's first son, named Doud Dwight and nicknamed "Icky," was born. When Icky was three, he contracted scarlet fever. Within a week he died. "This was the greatest disappointment and disaster in my life," Ike later wrote, "the one I have never been able to forget completely."

The Eisenhowers' second son, John Sheldon Doud, was born in 1922.

ICKY, 1920

In 1914 the First World War began in Europe. Three years later the United States entered the war and Eisenhower was anxious to go overseas. "A soldier's place," he once wrote, "was where the fighting went on." But he was kept in the United States. He was sent to bases in Georgia, Maryland, and Pennsylvania, to help train soldiers for battle.

At Camp Meade, Maryland, 1919

GENERAL FOX CONNER

After the war he served as an aide to General Fox Conner, "one of the Army 'Brains,'" Eisenhower later wrote, "a natural leader and something of a philosopher." Conner was sure that soon there would be a second great war. He told Eisenhower to be ready for it.

Eisenhower took Conner's advice. He attended the Command and General Staff School and finished first in his class. Next, he went to the Army War College and was rated a superior student.

In 1933 he was assigned to Douglas MacArthur, a colorful, brilliant general, first in Washington, D.C., and then in the Philippines. "This is the best officer in the U.S. Army," MacArthur wrote in his report on Eisenhower. "When the next war comes, move him right to the top."

IN THE PHILIPPINES
EISENHOWER IS SECOND FROM RIGHT, GENERAL MACARTHUR THIRD FROM RIGHT.

The next war *was* coming.

During the 1930s, Japanese forces invaded Manchuria and China. Italian forces attacked Ethiopia. The Germans took a section of western Czechoslovakia. Then, on September 1, 1939, German forces attacked Poland. Two days later Great Britain and France declared war on Germany. Eisenhower was serving in the Philippines. He was sent back to the United States. "I was certain," he later wrote, "the United States would be drawn into the whirlpool of the war."

In September 1941 he was chief of staff of the Third Army, for the Louisiana Maneuvers—"war games." His bold strategies were a great success. When the maneuvers were done, he was promoted, made a brigadier, "one-star," general.

On December 7, 1941, the Japanese attacked the American naval base and other military installations at Pearl Harbor, Hawaii. The United States was at war.

PEARL HARBOR, HAWAII, DECEMBER 7, 1941

Eisenhower was ordered by General George C. Marshall, the U.S. Army Chief of Staff, to report immediately to Washington to serve in the War Plans Division. "I've heard you like to make your own decisions," Marshall told Eisenhower. That's what he needed. Marshall said, "I want to see the solutions, not the problems."

Marshall took note of Eisenhower's abilities at organization, planning, and working with people. In June 1942 he put Eisenhower in charge of American forces in Europe.

GENERALS EISENHOWER AND MARSHALL IN NORTH AFRICA, 1943

From left to right, Generals Dwight Eisenhower, George Patton, Omar Bradley, and Courtney Hodges in Germany, 1945

Those were "sober, even fearful" days, Eisenhower later wrote. "Allied fortunes were at low ebb." But he would not consider defeat. He called the enemy completely evil. With them, he wrote, "no compromise could be tolerated."

Eisenhower was tough. He sometimes lost his temper. But he was also warm, honest, and sensible. He was able to get many strong-willed military people to work together. He got things done.

Eisenhower led Allied forces to victories in North Africa, Sicily, and southern Italy.

In December 1943 President Roosevelt named him supreme commander of the greatest combined land and sea wartime operation in history. It was a mix of troops, ships, and planes. It would cross the English Channel and fight the Germans first in France and then in Germany. The operation was code-named Overlord.

D day, the start of the attack, was June 6, 1944.

The "hopes and prayers of liberty-loving people everywhere march with you," Eisenhower told his troops. "The eyes of the world are upon you."

By the end of the first day more than 150,000 American, British, and Canadian troops had landed in France. In all some 3,000,000 Allied soldiers, sailors, and airmen were involved in Operation Overlord.

"People of western Europe!" Eisenhower announced on D day afternoon, "a landing was made this morning on the coast of France by the Allied Expeditionary Force. . . . The hour of your liberation is approaching."

WITH PARATROOPERS JUST BEFORE D DAY INVASION, JUNE 5, 1944

ALLIED TROOPS LAND ON THE COAST OF FRANCE

PRESIDENT OF COLUMBIA
UNIVERSITY, 1948. WIFE, MAMIE,
AND SON, JOHN, ARE IN THE FRONT
ROW. MAMIE IS ON THE AISLE.
JOHN IS AT HER RIGHT.

Operation Overlord was a great success. By mid August 1944 Allied forces were moving across France. By the end of the month Paris was taken. In May 1945 Berlin was taken and the Germans surrendered. Later that year Eisenhower was made chief of staff of the U.S. Army.

General Eisenhower retired from military service in 1948 to become president of New York's Columbia University.

Dwight Eisenhower was still immensely popular. People knew him to be honest and sincere. They loved his broad smile and some wanted him to run for president in the 1948 election. Eisenhower wasn't interested. "My decision to remove myself completely from the political scene," he wrote in a letter, "is definite and positive."

In 1950 he returned to military service to become the first military commander of the North Atlantic Treaty Organization (NATO). He was appointed by President Truman.

There was a call for Eisenhower to be the Republican candidate for president in the 1952 election. This time he decided, he later wrote, to "abide by the decisions of my party."

It seemed "I Like Ike" campaign buttons and posters were everywhere. In July he was nominated as the Republican candidate for president. In November he was elected the thirty-fourth president of the United States. He was reelected four years later.

1954

In January 1953, when he took office, American forces were fighting again, this time in Korea. President Eisenhower worked quickly to make peace. He was a soldier who hated war. "Every gun that is made," he said, is a "theft from those who hunger and are not fed." He kept the United States out of war during his remaining years in office.

President Eisenhower's "atoms for peace" program helped other countries find peaceful uses for atomic energy.

During his presidency, a system of superhighways and the space program were started. Taxes went down and incomes went up. Millions of American families bought their first telephones and television sets. Alaska and Hawaii became the forty-ninth and fiftieth states.

CONFRONTATION OUTSIDE LITTLE
ROCK CENTRAL HIGH SCHOOL,
1957

President Eisenhower ended segregation in Washington, D.C. In 1957 he sent federal troops to Arkansas so nine black students could attend the all-white Little Rock Central High School safely.

"When I came to the presidency, the country was in a rather unhappy state," he said. "I tried to create an atmosphere of greater serenity." And he did.

FEDERAL TROOPS OUTSIDE LITTLE ROCK
CENTRAL HIGH SCHOOL, 1957

WITH PRESIDENT
KENNEDY AT CAMP
DAVID, MARYLAND,
1961

In January 1961, at the end of his second term, he retired to his home in Gettysburg, Pennsylvania, to his favorite pastimes: writing, reading, painting, and golf.

Our nation's new leaders came to speak with him. They asked his advice. He was a respected elder statesman.

In September 1955, during his first term as president, he had a heart attack and recovered. In November 1965 he had another attack and never fully regained his health.

PLAYING GOLF, 1958

AFTER SUFFERING FIRST HEART ATTACK, 1955

His mind was sharp. His voice was firm. But his body was frail.

Four years later, in a bed at Walter Reed Army Hospital in Washington, D.C., he spoke his final words. He said, "I want to go, God take me."

Dwight David Eisenhower, the man who led the free world in war and peace, died on March 28, 1969. Leaders from more than fifty nations came to his funeral.

Former President Lyndon Johnson said, "His death leaves an empty space in my heart." President Nixon called him "an authentic hero."

Dwight David Eisenhower had lived West Point's motto: Duty, Honor, Country.

FUNERAL, WASHINGTON, D.C.

IMPORTANT DATES

1890	Born in Denison, Texas, October 14.
1892	Family returns to Abilene, Kansas.
1911	Enters West Point Military Academy, June 14. Graduates, June 12, 1915.
1916	Marries Mamie Geneva Doud, July 1.
1917	Son Doud Dwight ("Icky") born, September 24. Dies of scarlet fever, January 2, 1921.
1922	Son John Sheldon Doud born, August 2.
1922–1925	Serves as executive officer to General Fox Conner.
1925	Enters Command and General Staff School, August. Graduates first in his class, June 1926.
1927	Enters Army War College, August. Graduates, June 1928.
1933–1939	Serves with General Douglas MacArthur, first in Washington, D.C., and then in the Philippines.
1941	Serves as Chief of Staff, Third Army.
1942	Named Commanding General, American forces, European Theater, June; Commander of Allied Forces in North Africa, November.
1943–1945	Serves as Supreme Commander of Allied Expeditionary Force.
1944	Allied invasion of Europe begins, D day, June 6.
1945	German forces surrender, May 7.
1945–1948	Serves as U.S. Army Chief of Staff.
1948–1950	President of Columbia University.
1951–1952	Military Commander of NATO.
1953–1961	Thirty-fourth president of the United States, first elected November 4, 1952.
1957	Sends troops to Little Rock, Arkansas, to enforce school integration.
1969	Dies in Washington, D.C., March 28.

WEST POINT
HONOR GUARD,
1914

AUTHOR'S NOTES

According to a report in the *New York Times* of the June 19, 1945, welcome of General Eisenhower, an electric "noise meter" measured the sound the crowd made as the equal of 3,000 claps of thunder all crashing together. The New York City police department first estimated the crowd at 6,000,000 and later reduced the number to 4,000,000.

The seven Eisenhower sons were named Arthur, Edgar, Dwight, Roy, Paul, Earl, and Milton. Paul died of diphtheria before his first birthday.

Eisenhower was first named David Dwight, after his father, but soon after his birth his mother recorded his name in the family Bible as D. Dwight. She called him Dwight so there would be no mix-up between her family's two Davids and because David could be shortened to Dave, and she hated nicknames, including "Ike." In school Edgar was "Big Ike" and Dwight was "Little Ike," but not to their mother. If she heard someone call one of her boys Ike she asked, "Ike? Who's Ike?"

D day was first scheduled for June 3, 1944, but stormy seas forced postponement.

Eisenhower called the German Nazi regime "completely evil." If proof of that was needed, it came in May 1945 when he saw a death camp where Nazis killed people because of their race, religion, and politics. "The verbal testimony of starvation, cruelty and bestiality were so overpowering as to leave me a bit sick. . . . I made the visit deliberately, if ever, in the future, there develops a tendency to charge these allegations merely to 'propaganda'." He telegraphed George Marshall that he made these visits "in order to be in a position to give *first hand* evidence of these things."

In 1952 Eisenhower's campaign slogan was I Like Ike. Four years later it was I Still Like Ike. In both elections he ran against Democrat Adlai E. Stevenson. Eisenhower won with more than 55 percent of the total vote and 39 of the 48 states in 1952, and more than 57 percent of the vote and 42 states in 1956.

SELECTED BIBLIOGRAPHY

Ambrose, Stephen E. *The President*. New York: Simon and Schuster, 1984.

——. *The Supreme Commander*. New York: Doubleday, 1970. Reprint, Jackson, MS: University of Mississippi, 1999.

Brendon, Piers. *Ike: His Life and Times*. New York: Harper, 1986.

Eisenhower, David. *Eisenhower At War*. New York: Random House, 1986.

Eisenhower, Dwight David. *At Ease: Stories I Tell to Friends*. New York: Doubleday, 1967. Reprint, Fort Washington, PA: Eastern National, 2000.

——. *Crusade in Europe*. New York: Doubleday, 1948.

——. *In Review: Pictures I've Kept*. New York: Doubleday, 1969.

Gruber, J. Richard, with Dennis Medina. *We Like Ike: The Eisenhower Presidency and 1950s America*. Wichita: Wichita Art Museum, 1990.

Morin, Relman. *Dwight D. Eisenhower: A Gauge of Greatness*. New York: Associated Press, 1969.

Perret, Geoffrey. *Eisenhower*. New York: Random House, 1999.

RECOMMENDED WEB SITES

www.whitehouse.gov/history/presidents/de34.html
www.history.cc.ukans.edu/heritage/abilene/ikectr.html
www.eisenhower.utexas.edu
www.mcadams.posc.mu.edu/ike.htm
www.dwightdeisenhower.com